# Where in the World is God?

# Where in the World is
# GOD?

*Reflections on the Sacred Mystery*

## Kenneth J. Dale

RESOURCE *Publications* · Eugene, Oregon

WHERE IN THE WORLD IS GOD?
Reflections on the Sacred Mystery

Resource Publications
An Imprint of Wipf and Stock Publishers
199 W. 8th Ave., Suite 3
Eugene, OR 97401

www.wipfandstock.com

PAPERBACK ISBN: 978-1-7252-5220-2
HARDCOVER ISBN: 978-1-7252-5221-9
EBOOK ISBN: 978-1-7252-5222-6

Manufactured in the U.S.A.                                              DECEMBER 2, 2019

*This book is dedicated to all
who wonder about God*

# CONTENTS

# PREFACE

The writings in this little book are "mini-essays" or "poems," each one separate and complete in itself, written at different times. I make no claim to being a poet writing as a true "wordsmith," but neither have I confined myself to ordinary prose, except in the introductory pieces at the beginning of each section. This model has given me the freedom to write more freely in suggestive fashion rather than being tied to logical development of every idea. I request the reader not to read many of them in succession at one sitting; it will cloy you. But I hope these bits will, in the end, become a bottle of "new wine" with a sparkle of truth in our search for ways to think about God that are relevant to today's world.

There are five sections in this book. The first three sections look at God from various perspectives. The final fourth and fifth sections are different from the first three in that, despite questioning and probing, they call on the wisdom of biblical faith.

I am thinking especially of two groups of people as audience for this little book: those people, especially under the age of thirty-five, who live on the edge between the spiritual and the secular, respecting religion but often turned off by the church's blithe God-talk, feeling more and more at home with the "nones," and also those who may go to houses of worship regularly but who nonetheless struggle silently with the real meaning of God in their life.

A survey of current religious statistics shows a rapid decline in all religious affiliation,[i] with a concurrent interest in individual spirituality.[ii] This alarming situation in the church is a compelling factor that motivates me to write about God from a new perspective. Wrestle with me while I share my own deep questions, and new interpretations that I am finding helpful.

*Note: Even though the Bible speaks of God as male, and even though it makes for awkward sentences, I try to avoid the gender words, "he, him, his" with reference to God, inasmuch as God is above and beyond gender.*

Kenneth J. Dale, at Pilgrim Place

Claremont, California

Autumn, 2019

# ACKNOWLEDGMENTS

John Cobb and his influential Center for Process Theology have been a big factor in shaping my theology. I greatly appreciate his words of "orientation" to this book found on the back cover. I am also deeply grateful for the encouragement of Andrew Taylor, bishop of Pacifica Synod of the Lutheran Church in America to which I belong and for his words on the back cover.

I am indebted to those colleagues in the "Doing Theology" group at Pilgrim Place who have accompanied me on a journey from a narrow to a wider view of God. I cannot name all of them, but Charles Bayer's thoughts have been particularly stimulating. I am grateful to Bob Hurd, Bill Moremen, and John Denham, who gave advice and encouragement along the way, and to Rich Mayfield for our thought-provoking conversations and his stimulating critique of my work.

I also owe much to the many authors whose works appear in the Bibliography section, and to the editors at Wipf and Stock who guided me through the publishing process.

# INTRODUCTION

I constantly think about God, asking, Who is God? What is God? Where is God?

But who is so presumptuous as to write a book describing God, the infinite, ineffable God? But nevertheless, I want to write a book about God. I am aware of this irony, and to try to make an objective, accurate "description" of God, is folly, and definitely not the purpose of this book. Do not look for "proofs" for the existence of or nature of God. The best we can do is share our individual and communal *experience of God,* and the *belief in God* that arises out of that experience.

Knowing how many people hold what I consider inadequate beliefs about God, or have simply "given up on God" entirely, I feel a deep desire to share my own doubts and struggles and insights as I have probed the nature of God, which to me is a fundamental aspect of the spiritual life.

I write these lines being aware of the profound changes taking place in the modern and post-modern world views with respect to the concept of God. Since the 19th century, philosophers, theologians, and scientists, such as Friedrich Schleiermacher, Karl Marx and Charles Darwin overthrew traditional world views. In the early years of the 20th century "death of God" theories—think Altizer, Hamilton, and their popularizer, John Robinson (*Honest to God)*—grabbed the attention of many. In one sense, they were a reprisal of Dietrich Bonhoeffer's earlier call for a "religionless Christianity." These influential thinkers make it imperative that Christian theologians and church professionals be keenly aware of these changes in order to address today's listeners with a message that meets their mind-set.

Currently religious thought has rightly turned its energy toward matters of God in the context of social injustice. Despite there being ample justification for that, I still do not want to neglect the theological foundation for these concerns, which is, I believe, ultimately the One we call "God" and the way God works in the world.

I am aware that the subject of God can be approached in various ways: looking at comparative concepts of God in the various religions, or looking at God from the standpoint of philosophy; i.e. examining the classical ontological, cosmological, or teleological "proofs," of the existence of God, or learning from some of the prominent thinkers listed above.[iii] Currently, Fundamentalsts and most Evangelicals totally accept an image of God as an all-powerful Being existing in a place called heaven, distributing rewards for the good and punishment for the bad, especially on "Judgment Day." It's all "in the Book" for them, and they resist a questioning attitude.

But, although I am indebted to some of these for helpful insights, I am not writing from an academic angle, but principally on the basis of my own insights and experiences. Although I am already on the far end of my "mature years," I do not apologize for being a persistent seeker as long as I live. I follow David Brooks, a contemporary author, who recently commented, "You have to put yourself in this book."[iv] I invite any and all who are curious enough about God to put themselves in this book with me for a while and have a dialogue about God.

# ENDNOTES FOR THE PREFACE
# AND INTRODUCTION

i.      Here are some statistics indicating trends during the past 15 years in the United States, compiled by ABC News/Washington Post polls of over 174,000 random-selected telephone interviews conducted from 2003 to 2017.

- Christians overall in the American population are down from 83% of adult population in 2003 to 72% in 2017.

- Protestants are down from 50 percent in 2003 to 36 percent in 2017. Self-identified Catholics held relatively stable at 22%.

- During that time, people with no religion (the so-called "nones") have nearly doubled: 12% in 2003 to 20% in 2017.

- Among young adults (ages 18-29) during that time there has been a 16% increase in the "nones," climbing from 16% in 2003 to 35% in 2017.

According to surveys, one-third of undergraduate students wrestle with some kind of mental health issues, struggling with meaninglessness, asking "Why should I live?" Ten percent of those students struggle with thoughts of suicide.

ii.     There is another significant set of statistics that measure the numbers of people in the category we know as "spiritual but not religious." Consider the following statistics from a 2017 Pew Research Center's "Religious Landscape Study" posted on the internet:

- About 20% of all polled were unaffiliated with any religion, but 37% of these claimed they were spiritual but not religious.

- Another Pew Research reported in an article in the Los Angeles Times, July 13, 2019, by Varun Soni, dean of religious life at University of Southern California states that 20% of all Americans put themselves in the "spiritual but not religious" category. This includes the broadest spectrum of demographics—age, gender, race, etc. One-half of these identify as Christian.

iii.    See Lloyd Geering, *Reimagining God,* Part II.

iv.    Quoted from a review of David Brooks, *The Second Mountain*, in The Atlantic by Peter Wehner.

# I.

## IS A NEW PARADIGM POSSIBLE?

*The starting point for our adventure in trying to talk more meaningfully about God is to confront dissatisfaction with traditional talk, both on the street and in the church. Under the rubric of* Theism *the common conception of God as the all-powerful One like a super-human being seated in heaven, who controls the world but occasionally intervenes in our space, or simply as the "Man upstairs" is completely mistaken, if not idolatrous.*

*Unanswered prayers and the experience of man-made and natural catastrophes become the basis for disbelief in God. This was/is the experience of people all over the world when they reflected on the German holocaust in the 1940's. If there is a good, powerful God, how could such a God possibly let Hitler murder six million Jews, let countless thousands of children around the world die of hunger, or let hundreds of people be swept into the sea because of a tsunami?*

*It is my deep desire to speak meaningfully to today's religious seekers. We who are not content with talk about God as an all-powerful Being in the heavens must find new ways of conceiving of God that are more meaningful to our time. We begin in section I. with the negative and proceed to more positive approaches in later sections.*

# GOD, WHY ARE YOU HIDING?

I am not a philosopher, nor do I intend to address philosophers.

But we cannot avoid trying to dig deeper into realms of wisdom and truth.

That is what philosophy does for us,

and that is why people like me write books.

Philosophers are greatly concerned about God.

They ask whether there is any *reality* to which the word "God" refers,

or is this, after all, a creation of human imagination? [i]

People of our time ask, "Show me the evidence before I believe anything."

Yet no one in human history has yet seen God, so where is the evidence?

Can we worship and trust in something which remains an Unknown?

God is a hidden God even to writers of the Bible.

These dramatic words from a Psalm in the Old Testament still speak:

"How much longer will you forget me, Lord? Forever?

How much longer will you hide yourself from me?

How long will sorrow fill my heart day and night?"[ii]

This impassioned cry might well be ours.

If there is a God, why does that God so thoroughly hide from us?

Yet, despite all these negative experiences, why do so many people,

people around the world of almost every religion,

still persist in seeking and praying to God?

These are some of the problems that thoughtful people

have struggled with through the centuries,

and we are still engaged with them today.

# CHANGING HORIZONS

The majority of people on the street, and people in the pews of churches
    seem content with the traditional understanding of God,
      developed in ancient times when a "three story universe" was assumed.
      God was a supremely powerful Being existing somewhere in the "top story."
Creeds of the church attempt to define God more and more precisely,
    hoping that this will clarify Christian faith.
But currently there is turmoil in theological circles over notions of God.
    We have gone through an era in which "The Death of God"
    swept the theological world.

A current theologian, Karen Armstrong, finds that
    what unites sincere people of all religions is *compassion*.
She and others say that if the essence of religious faith is compassion and love,
    and if we live by love, then what is the need for assuming that
    someone called God exists outside of the reality of love itself?
A thoughtful friend of mine says, "Why do we cling desperately to language of
    metaphors and symbols that speak to a different age . . .
    a different way of understanding reality? . . .
    It just may be easier to be a devoted disciple of Jesus without believing in God."[iii]

We are all looking for a new paradigm relevant to contemporary seekers,
    pinpricks in the darkness for understanding "the God Nobody Knows,"[iv]
    not a rerun of the "church-talk" by and large unchanged for centuries.

# GOODBYE TO THE "GOD UP THERE"

I recently had an ah-ha! moment which spoke loud and clear:

    We *must* get rid of that image of God

    as someone somewhere "up there."

I have come to realize clearly that if God is in the category of "someone up there,"

    such a god is a limited being and not the true God at all,

    simply one among many gods, and to worship that one is like worshiping an

    idol, for that "someone up there" is a mental image of our own creation.

We must distinguish between "god" and "God."

    The challenge for us is to be open to new perspectives on "God,"

    the One who ultimately is not subject to definition or mental imaging.

This is where the medieval Meister Eckhart's famous paradox, "God, rid me of God,"

    begins to make sense. He implies two meanings of the word "God."

We are told that among 19th century Russians there were "hole-worshipers" who

    worshiped the void—holes they made in the wall—rather than any divine object.

    This freed them from having to make any specific description of God.

This may be extreme, but perhaps it is better than talking incessantly about God

    as though we knew her/him as a neighbor down the street.

# A LITTLE INTERCULTURAL INTERLUDE

We lived in Japan for many years, where the culture is imbued
    with an unusual religious situation.
The majority of the population claim some, usually nebulous, traditional affiliation with
    both Shintoism and Buddhism, but whose everyday life is simply secular.
Shintoism is the ancient national religion. It can be called pantheistic:
    countless shrines, large and small, dot the landscape.
    Each is dedicated to some part of nature or humanity.
The object of worship might be a beautiful mountain, or a gigantic tree, or the spirit
    of some deceased local hero—or it can be the emperor of the nation.
So we lived with pantheism in Japan, admitting both its negative side—
    the primitive worship of inanimate objects or national entities—
but also its positive side—a deep appreciation of nature,
    and in some sense a feeling of mystical oneness with nature.

But we also lived with Buddhism and its many elaborate temples
    where people of the neighborhood went to participate in rituals
    for the deceased, both at the time of death and at set periods after that.
Americans tend to identify Buddhism with Zen and meditation practices,
    but the latter are only one facet
    of a much more elaborate system of thought and practice.
What concerns us here is the Buddhist notion of God,
    which is essentially atheistic. The many Buddha images are not gods.
The Buddha symbolizes the attainment of enlightenment,
    toward which Buddhists strive.
This is a here and now "salvation"—a state of the self, not a relation to God.

In this paradoxical milieu, the representative of theism is Christianity,
    worshiping *chichi naru Kamisama*—the "Father God."

I wonder how much of the Shinto god concept

　　　and the Buddhist enlightened self concept

　　　still colors, perhaps subconsciously, the concept of God for Christians.

# PARADOXICAL, MYSTICAL GOD

More and more I have come to understand God in a mystical, paradoxical way:

    God exists in my awareness, in my consciousness,

    but is at the same time more than my consciousness.

God is an integral part of human life, but is not restricted to human life.

    God is in nature, pervading the whole natural world,

    yet not confined to nature.

These paradoxical words offer at least a starting point in knowing God

    by insisting that God is *not* a Being existing in some space "out there."

    How hard it is to erase this image of God

    as a heavenly, kind, old grandfather!

Yet for me, this is the first step in searching

    for a new paradigm for understanding of God.

    We need to be humble and open our minds to entirely new ways of thinking.

God's existence is far more incomprehensible

    than traditional images suggest.

I am convinced that God is somehow mysteriously

    in, with and under the whole of creation,

    including "nature," including humanity.

# THE INEFFABLE VS. THE IDOL

"God" can be an idol, when we think of "God" as an exotic "Somebody,"

    or as a majestic and powerful Being in the heavens,

    or as someone or something whose action

    we can direct by our ardent prayers.

The true "God" is beyond any object,

    is beyond any figment of our imagination,

    yes, is absolutely incomprehensible to the human mind.

Yet our human minds and emotions need something

    other than "the Incomprehensible" or "the Unknown"

    to worship and trust and enjoy.

That's why I am using the word "God," but using it with quotation marks.

    They symbolize this ineffable Being,

    the Being that is more than a being.

This is the Ground of all beings, the ground of all that exists,

    the fulfillment of the highest longings of humankind.


This is the One whose name the ancient Hebrew people would not even pronounce,

    the One held in such awe and reverence that the name could not be written.

    For them it was an "abomination" to worship anything other than the Ineffable.

We can only say what God is not; we cannot say what God is.

    To capture the Ineffable and name it

    and tame it as "God," is to make it an idol.

# NEW WINE SKINS FOR NEW WINE

Jesus, bringer of a truly new message, once told his followers,

    "No one pours new wine into used wine skins, because the wine will

    burst the skins, and both the wine and the skins will be ruined.

    Instead, new wine must be poured into fresh wine skins."[v]

    I am constantly searching for new wine skins.

These current concepts may be a bridge

    to bring the secular, the young, the thinkers of any age

    into a dialogue about religion.

We need to rethink our image of God and not let

    our God concept be "in the image of man."

It is our challenge to ponder the meaning of human beings

    made "in the image of God."

This is indeed "new wine"

    and needs new wine skins, new verbal concepts to accommodate it.

*[handwritten margin note: outdated ex, or tradition]*

# A RADICAL SHIFT

Look at the religious books on my reading shelf:

    *Jesus' Abba* (Cobb), *When God is Gone, Everything is Holy* (Raymo), *The*

    *Uncontrolling Love of God* (Oord), *Transforming Christian Theology* (Clayton),

    *God in an Age of Atheism* (Schilling), and more.

All fairly radical theologies for a person who has not considered himself a radical,

    but they are writers trying to find new ways of looking at the meaning of God.

At this stage in my own search for the meaning of Christian faith

    these books are not tempters leading me into faithless doubting,

but friends in guiding me into ever deeper understanding

    of the physical, intellectual, spiritual universe in which we live.


If we believe that God is not a separate being residing somewhere in the universe,

    but rather is in everything, in me, and in the universe as God's "body,"

    then we must find new language to handle such traditional concepts as:

God sent God's Son down to earth;

    Jesus ascended to the right hand of the Father;

    we die and go to heaven to be with God, to name a few.

The problem is that the "Someone up there" concept

    has been bred into most of us since childhood, and, if not intellectually, it

    emotionally sticks with us.

I call it my "Sunday School religion."

    For me, shedding that concept demands nothing less than

    a radically new paradigm for my faith.

# I MEET GOD IN MY FRAIL BODY

If the material/spiritual world is not something separate from God,

    but is the very place and stuff where God is,

then it follows that to honor God and hallow God's name

    I should not try to concentrate on some celestial Being,

    but focus on the things close around me, on the work I am doing,

    and not least on my own body.

For if I don't meet God here, I meet God nowhere!

    If God's Spirit is not embodied in *my body,*

    it is not the everywhere present Reality that I believe it is.


This is not pantheism, in which God is identified with material things,

    We recognize a *distinction* between God and the world, but not a *separation.*

The Spirit needs a vessel to give form to the formless, and my physical self is the most

    available vessel. Significantly, St. Paul admonished his friends with these words:

"Surely you know that you are God's temple and that God's Spirit lives in you!"[vi]

    God is in the natural processes, including the human birth and death cycle.

God is here suffering with us in our sadness, and taking delight in what we delight in.

    And this infuses life with meaning, and with peace knowing "all is well."

*[handwritten margin notes: "active verbs → actor", "Does this God have feelings?", "What does this phrase mean to you"]*

# BEYOND EVOLUTION

Many modern people see no need for God because

> evolutionary theory answers all the questions about the
>
> beginning of life and its many "miracles."
>
> But why cannot belief in God and in evolutionary theory exist together?

Evolutionary theory does not answer prior questions such as:

> If it all started with the Big Bang,
>
> from where did the energy of the Big Bang come?

Why is there the universal phenomenon of gravity in the solar system?

> What is the origin of consciousness?
>
> If galaxies are still multiplying, is there no limit to growth of the universe?

Without these amazing phenomena,

> there would be no world as we know it.
>
> There would be no human existence.

So where shall we go to answer these questions?

> Certainly not to a God whom we conceive of as
>
> a kingly Being reigning over this material universe by divine fiat,
>
> commanding stars to be born and human beings to behave,
>
> or else become the objects of God's punishment.

# PERMISSION TO QUESTION GOD

God cannot be hurt! God has no need to be defensive.

If God is truly the ineffable "All in all,"

    then God is Reality itself, Truth itself.

No amount of questioning on our part can hurt such a One.

    and we are free to ask questions

    of traditional doctrines, and of the Bible from whence many of them come.

I believe the Bible is a sacred book with a unique and wonderful message

    about God's amazing grace and love for humanity.

But to say that every sentence and every word are

    the words of God to us today is saying too much.

That is bibliolatry, worshiping a book rather than the divine Spirit

    which cannot be confined to a book,

    which is still speaking.

# THE HEBREW EXPERIENCE OF "YHWH"

I, along with the ancient people of Israel, believe the true nature of God

    is that invisible, intangible Force at the heart of all creation.

Paganism is worshiping an individual, tangible part of the universe.

    It is so natural to want to worship something tangible.

But from earliest Hebrew history an unseen Voice

    spoke to the ones who were especially called to hear it.

In the narrative of the call of Moses[vii]

    to become the one to lead the people of Israel out of bondage in Egypt,

    that Voice, in response to Moses' cry for clarity about the call,

    proclaimed itself to be "I am who I am" or simply "I am."

The One who communicated that name to Moses completely forwent

    a great opportunity to give a convincing definition of the divine.

    I wonder if Moses was satisfied with this whiff of the Ineffable.

The word they heard commanded them to forsake

    the worship of all tangible objects

    and go deeper to worship that mysterious Presence.


And here is something to ponder: in reverence for that Presence,

    they did not even pronounce or write the name.

The name was spelled with consonants only—YHWH,

    no vowels, so no pronunciation.

It is the name that we glibly pronounce "Yahweh," or "God" today.

The standard usage of the male personal pronoun—"he" or "him,"

    encourages us to see God as a male figure.

But there is no male or female in the self-definition, "I am who I am."

That is why "gender free" translations of the Bible and hymns—

    unfortunately often causing awkward sentences (e.g., "God's self.")—

    is a contemporary movement in the right direction.

# REVERENCE FOR LIFE

If we believe there is a God and a heaven, *hell?*

    but if neither of these is in any certain "place,"

    then where can they exist?

This, of course, is an impossible question

    but one answer is in the self, my self, your self.

God in myself, heaven in myself.

    Is there any evidence that this is true? No.

    Is there any evidence that this is not true? No. *good*

How do we honor such a God?

    We honor God by honoring the Creation—our very selves,

    and also all animals and plants, all mountains and forests

    that have been given to us to make human life livable and meaningful.

Honoring— respecting, recognizing, appreciating, caring for,

    loving the world around us—

    these are all expressions of our spirituality.

Our spirituality can be fulfilled in many ways.

    One way is through our sensory channels, the five senses.

What we see, hear, touch, taste, smell around us and within us

    can be a constant celebration of life,

    as we stand in awe of our very existence.

Albert Schweitzer covered it all in his famous *credo:*

    True religion is *reverence for life.*

# EVIL—WHY? WHY NOT?

It is a perennial question for both philosophy and religion—

Why does evil exist?

If the creation was originally good, then where did evil come from?

Why didn't the almighty God prevent it?

The question becomes painfully urgent when we ask,

How could a good God allow the horrors of the holocaust,

the murder of six million Jews in a "Christian nation"?

Even the memory of this event opens deep wounds,

and causes millions, who have been taught that God is in control,

to decide to have nothing to do with God.

Such a god is more like a demon than a god.

Indeed, this is the basis for much atheism.[viii] — *I can imagine a world in which a benevolent God exists and yet atrocities happen, this doesn't seem contradictory to me.*

The gist of my answer to this unending quest runs like this:

Consider that God is not all powerful,

in control of everything that happens.

God is present in the midst of life but does not control it.

Human freedom can accept or resist that presence. *← exactly*

Although some people of religion would question this,

most of us, seasoned by the humanism of our age,

believe that *freedom, free choice*

is a natural endowment of all human beings.

Weakness and evil are

the essential back side of strength and goodness.

The human will to do good implies

a back side of the possibility of doing evil.

Therefore, both good and evil are

the constant companions of our behavior.

"Why evil?" is the wrong question.

"Why not evil?" may be an equally valid question.

That's just the way things are!

*3)*

# PARADOXES WITHIN GOD

We listened while a friend told of his struggle to accept the diagnosis of
  his wife's developing the dreaded Alzheimer's disease.
We faced the perennial question: If God is the almighty Ruler of the universe,
  and if that God is good, is love,
  why is there so much suffering in the world?
I pondered these ideas:
  God is awesome, but not almighty.    *God is not about control,*
                                        *but presence*
  It is not in God's power to control good and evil in the world.
  If God controlled all that happens, we would have no freedom,    *but also*
  but freedom is the most distinctive and precious aspect of the human race.    *Creation?*
                                                                    *seems*
The God who is majestic in creation—consider the galaxies, and the atoms—    *out of*
                                                                    *synch*
  This is the same God who walks with the weak and suffers with the suffering.

                                *our values of*
This is the unique core of the Christian belief in God.    *good and bad are not*
                                        *important to God?*
  The God of ecstasy is the God of anguish.
Glory and power and beauty are in God's nature
  while at the same time anguish and suffering are also in God's nature.
Is this absurd? Is this too paradoxical and irrational to justify belief?    *no,*
  Perhaps it was at this very point that the early "Church Fathers,"    *life is full of*
  pondering the nature of God, settled on the doctrine of the Trinity:    *paradoxes*
  the majestic Father, the suffering Son, and the ever-present Spirit—

The Trinity—one attempt to make sense of the paradoxical God.
  But more of that later.

# DANGER OF IMAGING GOD

It is difficult to believe in God because we try to imagine, or image God

    in some category that we can reasonably understand.

But that is useless!

    "God"—by the very definition of the word—defies all human categories

    of thought and reason and scientific analysis.

Let's try a different way of thinking about God.

    Although our sensory equipment is indeed marvelous,

    it is not the only avenue for meeting reality.


Intuitive and emotional experience also provide an avenue of knowing.

    Many realities do not come to us through reason or the senses,

    but through emotion or intuition or some mystical means

    or direct experience —think of the world of the arts.

These can be powerful experiences,

    like the experiences of loneliness, or love.

    These are not based on the five senses, but are powerful realities.

I believe that God makes God's self available to humanity

    in many and various ways.

in Control + observing
vs
not omnipotent

# NOT IN CONTROL BUT NOT ABSENT[ix]

Late in life I have come to agree with the statement that

    God is not the all-powerful Ruler of the universe,

    that God does not *control* the world or human life,

    determining events such as illness or accidents or wars,

    letting some die while letting others live.

If God controlled everything, there would be no evil in the world; but there is.

    I believe God has created a world that operates on its own internal principles,

    producing good events and bad events, often according to human behavior,

    often according to the necessary workings of nature, such as earthquakes.

This is simply the way free humanity is, the way the world works.

    Think "mass shootings;" God could not stop

    what someone in the human family decided to do.

We are on the wrong track to thank God for

    the "blessings" of good things that happen in our lives,

    as though they were special gifts given just to us;

also wrong to turn from God when bad things happen to us

    as though God got angry with us.


And we are also on the wrong track to think that God is, therefore,

    non-existent, absent from the world and human life.

The reasoning of some atheists, such as Richard Dawkins,

    looks scoffingly at "the God delusion" and says that

    religion is a worthless idea which has spread out of control.

My response to that is simply: "Call it delusions if you will,

    but I perceive there is an existential longing in all of us

    for something beyond the natural,

    a deep longing of the human spirit for its Source.

*[handwritten marginal note: why do you say that?]*

Is not this the "image of God" within us,

which cannot be erased?

*our imagination of God is this feeling*

# II.

## METAPHORS POINTING TO GOD

*This section II is geared especially toward those who find the very existence of God a stumbling block. We start with the hope and the assumption that although God cannot be known directly, our thinking can be stirred through metaphors which point to God. In the previous section we recognized the futility of imaging God as a being like the only beings we are accustomed to seeing, that is, a (male) human being, albeit an absolutely unique being who can do things no human being can do. So we call God glorious King, Almighty Lord, and similar human images. These are all human-like metaphors which restrict our understanding of the nature of God.*

*So the question we confront is: Is there an entirely different genre of metaphors which might open our mind's eye to see God as a completely different kind of entity, one that might utilize the science-oriented concepts of the twenty-first century? Hopefully, we might find at least the possibility of a God concept which is different from a strong man looking down from the sky. Are there metaphors that might touch the "hem of the garment" of the Holy One to get a glimpse into another world?*

# ON THE USE OF METAPHORS

What is a metaphor? It is a figure of speech in which one thing designates another,

  thus making comparisons between the two.

It is often said that all talk of God is metaphoric, *← does everyone agree with this?*

  for metaphor is the only way to express that which

  cannot be rationally defined or grasped.

The word "God" itself can be a metaphor, or a symbol,

  for what we have never seen,

  and that indeed is the way we have to continue to use that word.

If that is so, what does the word "God" actually symbolize?

  "Something than which nothing other is greater"? "Ultimate Reality"?

  Philosophical concepts are so abstract!


But the metaphors we are talking about

  are taken from common life as "fingers pointing to the moon."

In simple, concrete language, they point to ineffable things.

It is said there are 130 different metaphors for God in the Bible.

  We will leave that for Section V. and look here mainly at metaphors

  that arise in the contemporary, science-oriented world.

# AIR

We live our daily lives submerged in the material world,

    interpreted to us through our five senses.

Yet God is invisible and non-material—

    making the notion of God seem unreal to human senses.

There is a tension between the material and non-material worlds we live in.

    Most of us restrict ourselves to the visible world.

    but much of what we experience in everyday life is immaterial and invisible.

*not air, but experience*

Consider the air in which we are immersed.

    Air is absolutely invisible but absolutely real.

    Without air in our lungs we will die in a few minutes.

    Without oxygen (air) in our blood stream,

    our organs, and the brain quickly shut down.


Or consider how this invisible air is so substantive that

    it allows giant airplanes to take off the runway,

    and supports their flights for long hours at high altitudes at tremendous speed.


These simple thoughts make it possible for me to

    *make a place for an invisible God.*

*step 1*

# THE FISH POND

I stood looking at the many giant-sized gold fish

    swimming in the big pond of a Japanese garden.

Those fish know nothing but water; they don't drown in the water;

    They draw their nourishment from the water;

    they depend on the water to sustain their life; they love the water.

We swim in the ocean of God's presence; we can't escape it.

    The benevolent universe is where we live and breathe.

    Why should we try to escape it     *Why call it this?*

    or close our mouth and not let the nourishment flow in?

Water in the pond, like light from the sun, like gravity everywhere

    sustains life regardless of our opinion about it!

*God is that mystery which surrounds all of life.*

    It is up to us whether or not we acknowledge and enjoy it.

# ELECTROMAGNETISM

We are constantly submerged in invisible electromagnetic waves, radio waves.

To begin with, think of the everyday experience of 21st century people—

the constant use of television and cell phones

and wireless electronic devices of all kinds

which bring communications to us without ever being seen.

Think of those billions of "smart phones"—

yes, countless millions of them, in use all around the globe,

sending messages on electromagnetic waves, all at the same time.

They enable us to talk with a friend in Japan,

to send messages in Chinese characters,

to receive the living tones of symphonic music,

to read books on line, and so much more.

All tangible experiences from a little gadget held in the palm of our hand.

The world is in my hand—mind-boggling! *but comprehensible*

*Like God's universal immanence.*

And what makes these smart phones

able to do all the fantastic things each of them is capable of?

There's the "Cloud"—that vast invisible area of

coordinated internet wireless data in a "bank"

responding to those billions of calls from people

who are incessantly receiving services

from that mysterious bank of data.

This ocean of transactions is utterly invisible, utterly out of our grasp,

yet our whole civilization depends on its reliability.

*Like God's invisible transcendence.*

# GRAVITY[x]

*(handwritten: not a metaphor here)*

*(handwritten: also danger: metaphors are bad for convincing)*

Gravity is a metaphor which allows us to <u>hint at the nature of God</u>

   in a deep and meaningful way.

Gravity is an invisible force acting on a system

   which draws one object to another.

Gravitation is a "field" that shapes empty space and time in a certain way.

   It holds the planets in their orbits, and stars in their place,

   and thus "shapes" the universe, by "luring" rather than constraining.

Without gravitation keeping us always "feet down"

   we would be capriciously flying objects, creating chaos in space.

Yet it is absolutely invisible and intangible, almost always unheeded,

   by and large beyond the grasp of science,

   but absolutely inescapable.

Without gravity, the universe would disintegrate,

   would literally "fall to pieces."


Yet the question of just what gravity is, in and of itself,   *(handwritten: hmm)*

   leads even scientists to puzzle about the nature and source of this power.

One aspect of gravitation is understood as waves, which, my scientist friend tells

   me, are like waves occurring on a spider's web when touched,

   but they are not gravitational power in and of themselves.

Using churchly liturgies, people worship the One

   who is "seated at the right hand of the Father." (Apostles Creed)

Might we not do better to give recognition to the Energy

   that is here and now stabilizing us on planet Earth,

   holding earth and moon and planets in their orbits,

   and making it possible for human beings to stay "grounded"?


*Gravity is a figure of God's mysterious transcendent and immanent power.*

# LIGHT

One of the mysterious phenomena of the universe is light.

    What is light, anyway? We look at a candle, a light bulb, or the sun

    and see what we call light, which consists of light waves.

    If we were to dissect a beam of sunlight or the candle flame,

    would we find some essence called light? I think not. *yes, photons*

We know light by what it does to the things on which it shines.

    In the night a light makes invisible things visible.

So what has the light done to those objects to make them visible?

    Have waves come and changed the nature of the object?


And how is it that these waves can travel through millions of miles of blackness

    that separate the source of the light, the sun,

    from the earth objects which it lights up?

        *metaphor ?*

In the Scriptures, God, and also Jesus, are often described as "the Light."

    We cannot see the divine emanation, or waves of spirit.

However, there is ample data about what that divine energy does

    to the persons on which this emanation falls,   *what ?*

    creating the difference of night from day,


*The mystery of light suggests the divine mystery in the universe.*
       *is like*

# SOUND

The sound of a 100-piece orchestra, of a 100-voice choir

    singing in exquisite harmony,

    the sound of birds chirping in the morning,

    or the sound of a baby's first word—

    all these have power to inspire and incite us to joy.

What a force for happiness these are for both individuals and communities!

    Yet their music consists only of invisible waves

    of different length and timbre vibrating through the air.

Sound waves, like light waves, remind us of the power of the invisible.

    Both music and speech—"nothing but" sound waves woven together in a pattern

    are another of the mysteries of the natural creation

    which open the possibility of oral communication.


For those who have ears to hear it, the "Word of God" comes

    as a mystic communication from the Unseen.

The Bible is commonly called "the Word of God."

    Jesus himself is called the "Word of God."

"Word" obviously has a vital role to play in the nature of God.

    Remember a word is a sound, a sound with meaning.


*Beautiful sounds, meaningful sounds—echoes of God speaking.*

*[Handwritten annotations:*
*this is chance evolution of our brains*
*of interpretation*
*|| weak*
*does this want to say that God "speaking" holds meaning within us only as its bible, not through mechanistic scientific approaches?]*

31

*[handwritten: terminology]*

*[handwritten: let's talk about this word]*

# SPIRIT

*[handwritten: = consciousness]*

Consider the concept of "spirit" as we experience it moment by moment—

emotions, memory, reason, imagination, personality and more.

These constitute our invisible human nature, our ability to create, to love,

which we summarily call "spirit."

Spirit constitutes the very essence of human nature.

It is utterly non-material, even though it is somehow

inexplicably connected to the brain.

So is it not possible that there could be an unseen spirit

in the universe as well as in my body?—

a Spirit that is powerful, creative and loving?

This invisible essence is so mysterious and wonderful

that it is usually written with a capital S—the Spirit, or Holy Spirit.

Theologian Paul Tillich was prone to emphasize the integral relation

between "spirit" and "Spirit"—the human spirit and the divine Spirit.

Tillich would profoundly say that if we are careless about our own spirit,

we cannot appropriate the divine Spirit.

*The human spirit opens the door to understanding the Holy Spirit.*

*[handwritten: also maybe a questionable "metaphor"]*

*[handwritten: 5 parts of mental health + well-being]*

# AESTHETICS

Perhaps we have too exclusively resorted

    to the *truth* (cognitive) and *goodness* (ethical)

    approaches to thinking about God.

But might not our understanding of God be enhanced

    by approaching God from the angle of the aesthetic?

There is much religious talk about praising the *glory* of God.

    Glory speaks of beauty and ecstasy rather than reason or behavior. *hmm*

    Glory implies an aesthetic approach to the divine. *hmm not the approach I would imagine based on previous interpretations of God*

Those moments of experiencing

    a great choir, organ or symphony concert,

    or the fantastic beauty of cherry blossoms or dogwood trees in the spring,

    or snow on the mountain range—

These are like shafts of glory from heaven.

    Here, not truth or goodness, but beauty is revealing the "glory of God,"

    if we but have sensitive ears to hear and eyes to see.

For me, the feelings aroused by, and the subjective perception of beauty

    are closely akin to religious experience.

*The non-rational but intuitive experience of beauty*

    *can reveal the glorious nature of God.*

*does this belong here? perhaps: experiencing God*

# A HERE AND NOW ENCOUNTER

I am walking in the mellow atmosphere of this fall day—

    deep blue sky, dark green oaks, yellow-red leaves,

    snow-capped mountains behind.

I prayed for enlightenment at that moment: What, who, where, is God

    in the midst of this overwhelming beauty?

Suddenly, an intuition:

    Breathe in deeply the awesome beauty of this place, in this time!

    Here and now I am experiencing the glory of the divine

    revealed in the world around me!

Have you never had such an experience?


Where there is beauty, there is God. *but also everywhere + everything*

In everything which gives us a deep recognition of beauty

    the Divine is present, more obviously than in theological textbooks.

    For it is there that we see and hear the logic of the Incarnation, which means


*God in the flesh, i.e., God in the material world.*

# "BODY OF GOD"

Seeing the world as the "Body of God,"

    as theologian Sally McFague suggests in her book of that title,

    opens a new model for God.[xi]

    It makes God immediately close to the human family.

She posits that the universe is the visible manifestation of God.

    Seeing the universe itself as the very body of God is a bold metaphor.

    But it makes sense.


We see the whole creation as an expression of the divine self,

    making itself known through the world of material things.

The human spirit cannot be located within the body,

    yet is an inextricable part of the body.

Even so, the spirit of God cannot be conceived

    apart from the universe.


*Perceiving the world about us as the body of God*

        *constantly brings God into our awareness.*

I simply open my eyes and say, "God is here;

        I am embraced by a benevolent universe.

        This is fullness of life, here and now!"

# A FLAME

There is a great story in the second book of the Bible, Exodus,

    of Moses in the Sinai desert being called by God

    to free the Jewish people from slavery in Egypt.

God appears to Moses in a burning bush.

    A bush—the most commonplace, nondescript thing in the desert.

This story implies that God appears

    in the most unexpected places and speaks

    in the most unexpected events, and at the most unexpected moments.

But the story says the divine appearance was like

    fire in the bush—a flame—hot, powerful, uncontrollable,

    but also momentary, disappearing as quickly as it appears.

A flame cannot be grasped and held.

    You can see right through a flame—it appears to have no material substance,

    but it is dangerously hot!

*So with God: elusive, non-substantive, yet real "to the touch."*

How often we try to capture, preserve, or institutionalize

    the sacred moments of encounter,

    to encapsulate the ecstasy of a fleeting Presence in a form and structure!

*We feel the divine Presence, and then it disappears; we cannot grasp and hold it.*

Sadly, institutions—even the church—

    inevitably tend to stifle that wonderful Presence.

# THE SUN

Doing Qi Gong in a garden in the morning sunshine,
    I was enlivened as I scooped up the air with both arms,
    raising them high in adoration,
    then slowly lowering them in a gesture
    bringing down the grace of heaven.
Then I had to look toward the sun for certain movements,
    but it was impossible to look directly in that direction.
    Direct sunight pained my eyes; it blinded me.

The sun gives us many benefits;
    it is a constant source of energy and comfort for us.
    But to look at the sun directly is overpowering and blinding.
    What a great metaphor for the human encounter with God!

*The divine energy and love are always flowing out,*
    *but the Source can never be seen directly;*
    *It would be utterly overwhelming!*

# ENERGY AND SPIRIT ENTWINED

Breathing in the cool air on this moonlit evening,

    comfortably lost in the trees and bushes, the air and soil,

    wondering if there is life on other planets,

    I am flooded with the sense that all the majesty of nature,

    including my own incredible gift of self consciousness—

    all of this speaks the language of the divine, *is* divine.

Since Einstein's day, science has discovered that all material stuff is,

    in essence, non-material *energy*—an amazing discovery!

We're learning the amazing reality of atoms, electrons, quarks.

    Energy, spirit, Spirit—where do we draw boundaries?

    Will the "God-particle" be found by quantum physics?


Can we go beyond metaphor and say with one of my friends that

    "God is in all existence as the dynamic presence . . . .

    *God may be the energy in all things and in all events.*"[xii]

In this sense, God *is* the life of the whole universe.

The human task is to use this energy

    to give form and meaning

    to the energy that has been given to us.

# SEXUALITY

Recall these strange words of St. Paul in the New Testament:

".....A man will leave his father and mother and unite with his wife,

and the two will become one. (This) is a deep secret truth..,

which I understand as applying to Christ and the Church."[xiii]

Paul is saying that the physical unity of husband and wife is a metaphor

for the divine essence being embedded

in individuals and within the Christian community.

This relationship is so intimate that it can be likened to sexual intimacy—

the penetration of the divine essence

into human consciousness and relationships.

This is not a philosophical figure;

this is not about abstractions.

St. Paul was talking flesh, with all its desires and potentialities;

he was talking intimate relationship and the greatest acts of intimacy.

*This is surely a model of the peak experience of divine immanence.*

# THE MYSTERY OF CONSCIOUSNESS

Perhaps the most profound mystery of human existence is
    what we call "consciousness."
The plant kingdom exists by the mystery of life seen in growth;
    The animal kingdom exists by the mystery of life "on the move;"
Only human beings *know and reflect on the fact* they are growing and going.
    Consciousness is the seat of knowing, of remembering,
    of willing, of imagining, of planning,
    of loving, of regretting, of hoping, of feeling, of communicating.
    Yet have you ever seen that "seat"?

And one of the distinctively human, precious aspects of self-consciousness
    is conscience, the seat of the sense of right and wrong, of morality,
    the place where decisions are made
    that can save or destroy ourselves—and the world.
We might say lightly, "All this is merely the work of the brain."
    But where in the brain? We are told, "From the pre-frontal area,
    from the anterior area, from the posterior area," and so forth.
Yes, we see the folds and the gray matter in the mock-up of the brain.
But we must ask, Where is, and what is the process, the dynamism
    at work in human consciousness
    by which all this mental and spiritual work is carried out?

*Is this a human mystery, or the Sacred Mystery at work?*

# LIFE

We ask again, "Who, what is God?"

    Let us think about the concept of *life* itself, and go beyond metaphor to ask,

    "Could God be that very mystery we call "life"—

    human life, of course, but also all animal life and plant life—all life!

Radical? Yes, but the phenomenon of life itself

    is also radically incomprehensible, even to science.

Christians speak about God's "incarnation" in Christ—God appearing in the flesh—

    Without denying the uniqueness of Jesus, can we extend that to mean that

    God can be/is incarnated—"enfleshed"—in my human life?

    In all life in the universe(s)?

The phenomenon of all manifestations of what we call "life"

    is truly beyond comprehension—

    whether it be the sprouting of an acorn

    growing eventually into a mighty oak tree,

    or the formation of a human being from an egg and sperm,

    growing through nourishment under the operation of DNA,

    the growth of cells, muscles, bones, ears and eyes, and so much more!

*It is only the dullness or the indifference of our sensitivities that tempts us*

    *to take life in all its unfathomable mystery and diversity for granted.*

# "HEAVENLY FATHER" [xiv]

This phrase can perhaps be called the "standard" Christian expression for God,
  as found in the biblical perspective of section V, so I shall not steal it here.
However, it must be recognized that even this phrase,
  used so universally in traditional Christian vocabulary, is a metaphor.
It is <u>unthinkable</u> that God is actually a male person
  who fathered not only the human race, but also Jesus, and now
  lives in some physical space called "Heaven," which gives him his title.
Such a god could not be the God we are seeking in this writing,
  but a figment of human longing.

Ironically, these two words from the Bible understood literally and factually,
  have been highly influential in creating the God concept
  which we are questioning—God as a kindly old man up in heaven.
But actually, the concept of "father" is symbolic of
  love, of strength, of caring, of wisdom,
  and represents Source and Progenitor, that from which all things flow.

*"Heavenly Father" has profound meaning, but the words are metaphors.*

# III.

## GOD AS SACRED MYSTERY

*We started this writing on new ways to think about God with a focus on what God is not. I've been quite clear in stating what I believe are mistaken notions of a God "out there," but now it's time to look positively at the implications of God as Sacred Mystery.*

*We deliberately are avoiding the whole field of philosophy where the existence and nature of God have been the object of puzzlement and attempted explanation for thousands of years. This personal writing makes no pretense of examining or critiquing the classical arguments for the existence of God.[xv] In this section, I, influenced by many teachers and writers to be sure, want to share some of my own probings and experiences of the divine tap on my shoulder, with reflections based on them.*

Context of Jesus' life outside of patriarchal white archaeologists / biased

history of other religions, respect, and humility, development of Christianity

literacy + "other", narrative of progression

"He"

penetration / sexuality

# WHAT IS GOD?

For me, God is the invisible, indefinable omnipresent Spirit,
> ever creating, always loving the entire creation,
> and especially human beings, including myself.

But we can never define or know this God completely.
> We can only feel and intuit the divine presence which
> breathes out the breath of unconditional love.

# THE SACRED MYSTERY

I long for and seek daily for some "definition" of God,

    but not a general definition for all—

    that would make God the object of academic research.

But I search for an understanding that will be satisfying enough

    to allow my mind honestly to "worship Him in spirit and in truth."

After much struggling and juggling of words and anguished thought,

    presumptuous as it may be, I share the following descriptive words

    which allow me to think and speak of God without tongue in cheek:

*"God" is that Sacred Mystery hidden in the love*

    *known in the creative processes of the universe and human life.*

Or a variant might be:

    *"God" is holy Mystery, fountain of love and creativity.*

Or another variant: *"God" is the Sacred Mystery*

    *revealed in eternal love and creativity.*


These phrases hark back to earlier centuries, when Latin was used,

    and human beings stood in awe of the *mysterium tremendum et fascinans*—

    that intriguing, fascinating, holy otherness of the Sacred Mystery.


But these statements are awkwardly wordy, at least for everyday use.

    Is it possible to compress this into a single word for use in conversation or prayer?

Ironically, it is all but impossible to find such a word

    that communicates these thoughts and feelings,

    except the word G-O-D.

But "God," with its almost universal connotation of a human-like, almighty being

    that rules the universe, is the word I wish to avoid—a dilemma!

But granted this linguistic difficulty, when we do use the word "God," it should be done
with the understanding that there are three meanings of this word:

a god that is man-made,

a god that is like a Heavenly Superman,

and the God of Sacred Mystery.

When I say the word "God" in religious context, it is important that

I am aware of using the third meaning.

# THE ONE BEYOND SPACE AND TIME

The most inherent character of the universe as we know it

    and human life within that universe,

      is that we are creatures bound within *time* and *space*.

Stop and think a moment—can you imagine your existence

    apart from these two "givens?"

There is the time you were born and there will be a time for you to die.

    There is the space your body is now occupying,

      and the space between you and your next door neighbor,

      or between you and South Africa.


But sages and religions talk about an *eternal* God,

    and a God who lives "in heaven,"

      yet a God who is everywhere present.

In other words, they see God as that which is NOT bound by time or space.

    Indeed, if God is truly different from the human family,

      this very thing is what makes god God.

God is of a completely different order of things,

    an order where one can be everywhere at once,

      where one has no beginning or end.

If God's nature is truly hidden in a different order of things

    from what human beings can understand,

      then what can we do but stand in awe of this overwhelming Mystery!

Our theological dogma should be more tentative,

    more humble, more awe-filled.

# GOD AS "BEING ITSELF"

Since the time of Paul Tillich many have become accustomed to saying
    that God is not "a being" but "Being itself."[xvi]
If God were a Being, even though we write the word with a capital letter,
    God would be reduced to one being among other beings,
    one entity among other entities,
    and as such would not be God at all.

"Being itself" is another way of stating
    that God is the Ultimate universal Presence.
God is even beyond anything in the whole universe
    that humans can imagine.

If God is "Being itself," then God is in everything,
    every atom of every substance in the universe.
If God is in every atom of stuff, like it or not, I am already existing in God.
    God is breath of my breath, life of my life.

# "PANENTHEISM"

God is immanent in the world and the world is immanent in God.

    This is a central insight of so-called "panentheism".

Believing this, we can experience everything that exists as being a receptacle for God.

    It indeed counters the "God out there" concept

    so common in Christian tradition.

Panentheism sees God as both in the universe and transcending the universe.

Panentheism sees the world as part of God, but not the whole of God.

    It is different from pantheism,

    which sees God identified with the material world.[xvii]

This basic concept of panentheism has been

    a powerful influence in shaping theology

    and Christian ministry in this generation,

    and it has been a strong influence in shaping my own awareness of God.

For me, it brings God into my conscious awareness

    time and time throughout the day—

    within me, around me, under me, over me,

    between me and my neighbor

# GOD AS BENEVOLENT UNIVERSE

Our highest human capacity is self-consciousness.

    Since the creature cannot surpass its creator,

    the sacred Mystery too is, in some sense, self-conscious.

Our highest capacity within this self-consciousness

    is the experience of loving and being loved.

    So God must also have the capacity to love and be loved.

Concretely, how can we know that? What does it mean to say God loves us?

    Laying aside the Jesus event momentarily, I can give my own testimony:

When I am open to it, I am in touch with

    an overwhelming, comforting personal Presence

    that empowers me to live in inner peace and creativity and hope.

When I am open to it, there is an oceanic sense

    of a creative power in all nature,

    keeping the universe alive and keeping me living fully,

    a sense of outpouring love for everything and everyone;

    a sense of being enveloped by a benevolent, loving Universe

    full of beauty and potential power.

Is not this "Benevolent Universe" another way of saying "God is love"?

# WHERE IN THE WORLD IS GOD?

Watching the astronomy show at the Adler Planetarium in Chicago
>   filled me with an overwhelming religious emotion.

The mystery of the Creator grew deeper.
>   It was clear that the Christian God
>   cannot be a Being who exists somewhere "out there"
>   in that immeasurable vastness of unknown time and space.

If that is so, then, if God indeed is a reality, *where in the cosmos is God?*

Is mysticism the answer?—God identified with the human soul?

Or is traditional theism the answer—an omnipotent Being in heaven?

In my experience the fundamental mystery of God is found in
>   the simultaneous immanence and transcendence of the divine.
>   God of the universe and God of my heart—
>   that's really way far out!

But at this point I feel the truth of Meister Eckhart's words that
>   the more one tries to define the ineffable,
>   the less it actually is *ineffable.*[xviii]

# GOD AS "THE MORE"

I was deeply moved as we listened to the stirring music
    of the Mozart *Requiem* in Disney Concert Hall.
Why is it that in the midst of stirring beauty, we instinctively turn to praise?
    And why do we turn to prayer in times of anguish?
Is it not because when we experience great beauty,
    and also when we experience great pain,
    we are at the brink of realizing the boundaries of our own capacities?
In both cases we are at a point where reasoning cannot explain the experience.
    We are driven to something beyond reason, beyond ourselves,
    to the "More"—a word from the psychologist William James
    often used by theologian Marcus Borg.[xix]

How do we respond to this experience of the "More"?
    We sense it as something that stirs our spirit,
    something unspeakably awe-inspiring.
God is vastly greater than simply a "More" to our everyday experience,
    but it is a place to start, namely,
acknowledging that there is *more* to life than
    what we grasp with our five senses,
    that intuition is a valid way of knowing.

# GOD AS "THE OTHER"

In times of deep distress and despair the "God within" is not enough.

    At such times, being caught up in God's immanence

    simply absorbs God into my inner weakness and turmoil.

At those times I grasp on to the transcendent God

    who stands above my subjective darkness,

    who is described by voices from the past as

    "my Rock and my Refuge," or the "mighty Fortress."

And also described by modern voices such as philosopher Jean-Paul Sartre

    who spoke of the "God-shaped hole in our consciousness,"

    where people have always sought for the sacred,

    sought to draw upon the "Other power" in hope.


This is the God who is not just the comforting presence

    nestled in my psyche as part of my weak self,

    but the One who is totally "Other,"

    offering a saving hand when I long for that.

Again we encounter the ultimate mystery of the divine:

    both immanent and transcendent.

It is totally a "larger than life" compassionate Power

    that constantly empties goodness into my fragile, uncertain self.

The great "Other" becomes the "More" in me.

# GOD AS THE HOLY ONE

The first words of the Lord's Prayer give a clue about the God to whom we pray.

    In this prayer we do not ask God for or thank God for specific things.

The prayer does not visualize God as a kindly cosmic grandfather

    who hands out gifts and blessings if we but ask fervently enough.

    This makes a mockery of God, who is far beyond being such a gift-giver.

The first sentence of this prayer is, "Hallowed be thy name."

    This strange word reminds us that God is holy—

    that which draws forth our awe and adoration,

    numinous, transcendent, sublime,

    reminding us of the mysteries of the universe.


We have lost the sense of the numinous, the holy in today's secular world.

    TV and smart phones and newspapers consume us

    with their unceasing flow of unnecessary information.

Even religious talk seduces us with intellectual analyses

    of the sacred texts and rituals and traditions.

Where can we escape to revel in the silent experience

    of awe in the face of holiness?


The sense of holiness is at the very center of true religious experience.

    Ethics and morality, aesthetics and the celebration of life

    all bear a likeness to religion.

But where religion differs from them is

    in recognizing the priority of the sense of awe

    in the presence of the "hallowed name,"

    in the presence of the Sacred Mystery.

# AWAKEN TO SPIRIT!

The idea of the holy or the numinous is central
    in many religions, including Christianity.
It is that "Other," that unseen "More," the kingdom of soul
    which gives ultimate meaning to all our thoughts and actions.
Yet one's entire life can be lived oblivious to the Holy,
    disregarding it or rebelling against it.
That is why the "Hallowed be thy name" of the Lord's Prayer,
    and the "Do not take the name of the Lord in vain" of the Decalogue
    both stand as preludes at the beginning of their sayings.
That is, they serve as an invitation, saying,
    "Awake to the spiritual world around you, don't take it lightly!
    Acknowledge the Mystery that surrounds you!
    Respect, honor, and obey the holy Word that comes to you!"

# IS GOD PERSONAL?

For those who probe the cosmic dimensions of God's existence
one question always remains: Is God personal?[xx]
As personal beings we long for a personal God,
but how can that which is best described as a Mystery be personal?
Panentheistic concepts proffer a profound perspective—
God in everything and everything in God.
But such a God leaves us with ambiguity about how a God who is
in everything and everyone can at the same time be personal.

Personal ideas seem to throw us back into the traditional mold of theism—
a divine, benevolent Being watching over us, sometimes answering prayers,
sometimes not.
God can be confined to neither "person" nor "super-person."

However, if God is indeed, directly or indirectly, our creator,
God must be personal for I know myself as personal,
and the creature cannot be greater than the Creator.
Such a God is indeed a Mystery.
Perhaps the most profound thing we can do is
to surrender our person to the creating Mystery.

# JESUS AND HIS "ABBA"[xxi]

How shall we call on God?

Worshiping the Mystery might satisfy those who feel at home in mysticism.

　　But names such as "The Almighty," "Creator," "Lord" or "King"

　　might be preferred by many Christians as a term for God.

But why not first ask, What did Jesus call God? That should be a model for us.

*Here is a startling thing:* Jesus simply called this Holy One his Father!

　　Let's look at that word that is translated into English as "father."

　　It is the Aramaic word "*abba*."

　　(Jesus is assumed to have talked

　　with the common folk in Aramaic, not Greek.)

Significantly "*abba*" is a word that expresses great intimacy,

　　being a more familiar word than the Greek "*pater*" (father),

　　and more informal than the English word "father."

It is actually more similar to the English "papa" or "daddy."

How can we juxtapose impersonal qualities (mystery)

　　with very personal qualities (papa)?

　　What can we say but that we err when we try to pin down

　　the nature of God into one category,

　　or when we try to draw parameters around

　　that which has no parameter,

　　describe the indescribable,

　　or analyze what will always remain enigmatic.


For most of us who have had a good experience of "Daddy" or "Papa"

　　these words bring solid security and deep comfort.

# GOD: FATHER AND SOURCE

It hit me suddenly—the profound meaning of Jesus' calling God "Father."
   Why father? or mother? We experience parents as the source of life
   and the one who nurtures the created child with loving care.
Jesus saw God as his loving Source
   whom he could trust completely to care for him.

A colleague wrote a paper on near-death experiences,
   concluding that the great majority of those recorded experiences
   are the experience of "going home,"
   with the implication of going back home to the Source!
   Seeking their progenitor, as people today are seeking their ancestry.
We stand in awe of the Eternal Source,
   and feel nourishing paternal/maternal love
   flowing from that Source.

# EACH MUST FIND GOD

Is it heresy to suggest that each person

    can and must find Ultimate Meaning for her/himself?

    to suggest that every one of us

    must find our own path to the Holy Mystery?

Discovering the existential meaning of the Mystery is not something

    that comes from research,

    not from studying "right doctrine" from a book.

That discovery comes only after deep personal reflection and painful struggle

    through the valley of the shadow of nihilism.

    Finally the discovery surprises us *as a gracious gift*.


I will never know what "God" is to you

    and you will never know what "God" is to me.

The Voice of the Mystery speaks to each of us with distinctive tones—

    although religious adherents hopefully find

    a commonality in public liturgy and worship.


If we understand God's nature to be truly that of a Holy Mystery,

    theological dogma will be more open to alternative expressions,

    the teacher of doctrine more ready to listen.

The preacher will not preach in the tone of an academic,

    but in the awe-filled tone of a poet.

# THE IMPOSSIBLE QUESTIONS

Why do people get brain tumors in mid-life and tragically die?

    Why does a group of devout religious pilgrims

        meet instant death in a plane crash?

    Why are babies born with physical or mental disorders?

In times of deep distress we are forced into the experience of suffering and evil.

    We are confronted with vexing, enigmatic questions:

    If God is almighty, why does God allow such evil to take over?


To teach people that if only they pray and commit themselves to God,

    God will bless and care for all their needs is a false promise.

    This is one of the things that drives people away from God and church.

Naming God, or "God's will," or stating "God knows what's best"

    to answer these questions is meaningless,

    although it must be granted that such statements

    do bring comfort to some suffering people.


I believe the only valid answer is I don't know, we can't know.

    These experiences are our "given"

    in this world into which we were born.

Whatever is, whatever happens is our "given."

    If it's good, making the most of it gives meaning to life.

    If it's bad, making the best of it gives meaning to life.

In either case, depending on human openness,

    the Holy Mystery is there offering the comfort and hope

    that lies in the discovery of *meaning* for all life's experiences.

# THE DEEPEST MYSTERY

Have you ever gazed into the vast emptiness of the desert and mused:

"Why does humanity exist at all?

Why does the universe exist at all?"

It is not "necessary" that there should be any world or any human life.

Is it all just by a random evolutionary process after all,

from a spark setting off the Big Bang

to a universe of billions of galaxies?


But who ignited the spark? What is the origin of my consciousness?

Is the whole thing just a big nihilistic trick after all?

Or is there a "Sacred Mystery" that stands

prior to, beyond, and within all knowable existence,

before which/whom we can only bow in silence?

We are not talking simply about a mystery, the kind of "mystery"

we face daily when something strange that we can't explain happens.

No, Sacred Mystery as I use the term has a cosmic dimension,

It points to an awe-inspiring entity that is indeed holy.

It is an apophatic (unknowable) divine concept

which cannot be known by ordinary means.

# IV.

## A THREE-FACED GOD?

*From its earliest centuries, Christianity proclaimed its central belief in Incarnation, that is, God entering humanity in the person of Jesus Christ, and its consequent belief in what is called the "Trinity." Therefore, as a Christian, in doing any serious thinking about the nature of God I cannot escape the responsibility of taking this concept of Trinity seriously.*

*What follows is a series of reflections on how Christians have come to understand why God has traditionally been called the "First Person" of the Trinity, God the Father Almighty, why Jesus is called the "Son of God," the "Second Person" of the Trinity, and why the spirit of Christ is called the "Holy Spirit," the "Third Person" of the Trinity.*

*These themes have been dealt with in countless tomes of academic Christian theology. But the academic approach to the Trinity often leads us not to a richer understanding of the mysteries of God, but simply to more intellectual complexities. I would again like to use my own experience as a base for considering some of the distinctions within the divine work we experience, without dividing up God into "three persons."*

# THE TRINITY—WHAT IS IT?

Did you ever wonder about seeing the triangle used as a Christian symbol?

    In some churches it often appears on altar cloths or pulpit hangings.

    There are historical and theological reasons

    behind this three-sided symbol.

Christianity holds to a "Trinitarian God."[xxii]

    "Father," creator of life—all life;

    "Son," Jesus, the outpouring of inclusive love;

    "Holy Spirit," sharing the divine Spirit with all creation.

All three of these are supreme mysteries.

    Life, love, spirit—these are all universals,

    but they find concrete expression in the Trinity,

    a term used throughout Christendom

    in spite of its not being a substantial biblical description of God.

Richard Rohr offers this concise, insightful description of the Trinity:

    Father—immensity.

    Son—immanence.

    Spirit—intimacy.

# WHAT! A THREE-FACED GOD?

Does "Trinity" mean that God is, after all, someone like a person,

    with a face, no, three faces, occupying their various posts in the universe?

    That would be making a farce of the concept of "Trinity."

For thousands of years religious thinkers have grappled

    with trying to understand the perplexities of God.

In their quest for understanding the nature of Jesus,

    the second and third century "Early Fathers" of Christianity settled on

    the doctrine we call "Trinity" as their key to interpreting the nature of God.

Stated in my simplified theology, they were trying to say that

    there are three distinct functions within the divine,

    three aspects of God's work.


They used the label *face* or *mask* which in their Latin language

    was the word *persona,* usually translated into English as *person.*

The word "persons" of the Trinity is, unfortunately,

    easily misunderstood as referring to three distinct individuals,

    whereas they were meant to point to three faces

    or facets of the divine being—

God the Father as the transcendental creator of the universe,

    Jesus the Son as a manifestation of the divine in history, and

    the Holy Spirit as the ever-present divine immanence in human life.

# GOD AND JESUS

Children sometimes are taught to pray to God,

    other times taught to pray to Jesus. Is that all right?

We are focusing on the nature of God in this writing.

    That is a good starting point for all persons of whatever faith.

For nearly all people seek after God in some manner,

    and it is hard to think of any religion without some deity.

But it is that man, Jesus, who is the focus of faith for Christians.

    How should we understand this unique person, hailed as the Son of God?

    How are Jesus and God related?


Many Christian theologians hold to a relatively simplistic view of Jesus—

    he was God in visible form—period!

Many "liberal" theologians through the centuries have also taken a simplistic view:

    Jesus was an ordinary, righteous man, a great teacher of wisdom.

Many atheists, wary of God, are admirers of, even devotees of Jesus.

    Richard Dawkins, who wrote *The God Delusion,*

    also wrote an essay entitled, "Atheists for Jesus."[xxiii]


Traditional orthodoxy tried to put the human and divine nature

    of Jesus Christ into brain-twisting statements about Jesus,

    such as the Athanasian Creed does. Here is a sample from that creed:

"He is God, begotten before all worlds from the being of the Father . . . .

    equal to the Father in divinity, subordinate to the Father in humanity.

    Although he is God and man, he is not divided . . . ."[xxiv]


But neither is Jesus an extra-terrestrial Being

    sent from outer space to show himself

    more powerful than other gods.

To believe in Jesus is to believe in the exciting possibility
of incarnation—God "enfleshed"—not just in Jesus,
but in myriad ways in the world.

# JESUS—NOT GOD, BUT WORD OF GOD

How many times did I hear the Sunday School children singing
    a little ditty that ended with "Jesus was God, you know."
Jesus was not God. The Bible never says he was God.
    To simply call him "God," is putting Jesus in a category
    of being another god in a plurality of gods.
The Bible says he was the "Word" of God, or the "Son" of God.
    These point to Jesus as the *logos* (Greek for "word"),
    i.e., the *expression* of God's nature.
What did Jesus's life express about God?
    That healing in the broadest sense—restoring things to their right condition—
    is the divine plan for the whole creation, especially for humanity.
That the true way of life for humanity is to show love for all people
    in a way exemplified by Jesus, who gave his very life for others,
and to be faithful caretakers/stewards of the whole creation
    which has been given to the human family to use and enjoy.

And Jesus was a teacher, both through verbal teaching,
    but more powerfully with the example of his life—
    a life of inclusive love for all people,
    a life devoted to walking humbly with God without hypocrisy.
It is better for people of religion not to spend their energy
    on analyzing historical documents stating the beliefs of our forefathers,
but to focus on what we *do* know now—
    this clear, practical Way of the Word.

# DEFINING JESUS? IMPOSSIBLE!

Jesus told a doubting Philip, "Whoever has seen me has seen the Father . . .

I am in the Father and the Father is in me."[xxv]

We tend to make these words preposterous

by imagining an almighty heavenly One

physically invading our planet

in the form of Jesus as a supernatural being.

But let's say it with a different accent:

Jesus says, "When you look at me—this real flesh and blood man—

you are looking at someone who acts out the character of God.

Look at my way of life and you are looking at God's character!

Follow me and you will understand God's Way."

But there is a paradoxical sequel:

Whenever I think I have the person of Jesus explained

to be human just like me, I recognize him as

someone quite beyond me,

quite beyond what any other man has been or said or done.

Even the most ardent spiritual seekers

will never be able to make a "definition"

of Jesus any more than they can define God.

# A NEW CHRISTOLOGY

When God is not conceived of as a "Being," but as a pervasive Sacred Mystery,
   Christology (teaching about Jesus) takes a loop!
For orthodoxy posits a trinity—Father, Son and Holy Spirit,
   and says, God sent his Son down from heaven,
   and drew him back to heaven.
A new "Christology" is demanded by new concepts of God,
   although the person of Jesus has always been
   a mystery to Christian thought.
Whatever might have happened "ontologically" at his conception and birth
   or at his baptism,
   I, nor anyone else, can know.

Presumptuous as it is, allow me to suggest
   some directions we might go here:
   Jesus was obviously a true human being, 100% human.
What made him unique is that he was completely
   open to the presence of God,
   obedient to the word of God in his heart.
   He surrendered himself totally
   to the will and way of God flowing into and through his life
   to the point where he was one with God.

He spoke truth to power, and exposed the hypocritical religious rituals
   which he saw being practiced in the Temple of his day.
For this kind of life and work he was hated by officials
   and finally killed in the cruel manner of crucifixion.
But his followers experienced his presence
   even after he had been killed.

They experienced his resurrection from the dead,
and came to call this mysterious resurrected person
the "the living Christ."
Yes, he was a one-of-a-kind person, the Son of God.

# BELIEVING IN JESUS MEANS . . .

"Believe in Jesus, and be saved!"

    What words are more bandied about in Christendom than these?


But what does that really mean anyway?

    What kind of a person was this Jesus in whom we are to believe?

Was he one, who, as many claim, was sent to the world

    to offer himself as a sacrifice for sin so God's wrath against sin

    could be mollified and we could go to heaven?

Many conservative Christians believe that today, as I did for much of my life.

    But now I see the whole drama of the Jesus's life and death differently.


Jesus, man of Galilee, saw himself as the one

    chosen in his baptism to live a life totally immersed in God,

    chosen to do divine works of love and healing in the world.

So to "believe in Jesus" is to believe, along with Jesus,

    that God actually is a living, loving One

    who is really alive among us,

    continually breaking into our human drama.


To "believe in Jesus" is to believe that God is a God who can be "incarnated,"

    who brings the spiritual into the material,

    the divine into a human body,

    and yes, into human bodies like yours and mine.

# HISTORICAL MYSTERY, MYSTERIOUS HISTORY

Traditional Christian theology says that Jesus was both human and divine.

As such, Jesus was a part of human history, but his divine nature is a mystery.

So how can "both divine and human" make sense, when they represent entirely different

worlds—the world of mystery and the world of history?

This is an age-old dilemma with no solution.

Volumes of theology books

have been written on Christology.


But, put very simply, Christians believe that, somehow,

in Jesus the eternal Mystery became historical reality,

and the historical Jesus embodied an eternal Mystery.

The rest is a puzzle, at least for now.

# JESUS OF HISTORY, COSMIC CHRIST

Theologians often draw a distinction between

    the "Jesus of history" and the "Cosmic Christ."

Jesus was a historical reality, but Christ is a cosmic reality.

    A portrait of the Jesus of history is drawn in the four Gospels,

    which are biographical works.

The concept of the universal Christ,

    especially found in Paul's writings in the New Testament,

    offers a different picture of Jesus.


The Gospels are narratives about the "pre-crucifixion" life and work of Jesus

    in the Palestine of his day.

The writings of Paul, and also the endings of the Gospels,

    show a different "post-resurrection" Christ

    who is not tied to history, but is a universal spirit in the whole cosmos.

Especially in the letters to the Colossians and Ephesians

    Paul presents Christ in the most exalted, cosmic, poetic terms—

    quite a different figure from the humble,

    suffering Jesus of the Synoptic gospels (Matthew, Mark and Luke).

Both the "Cosmic Christ" and the "Holy Spirit"

    convey God as a spiritual presence in the world today.

# A SECOND LOOK AT SACRIFICE (1)

Especially in the season of Lent, before Easter,

    Christians often contemplate the cross on which Christ was crucified.

    What happened on the cross?

    Why did the "Father" let his "Son" be killed?

There is a teaching called the "substitionary theory of the atonement,"

    which is ascribed to the Medieval bishop, Anselm.[xxvi]

It goes something like this: The human race is very sinful,

    so the good God necessarily vents

    his wrath and punishment on sinners.


Throughout history the Jewish people

    had offered animal sacrifices at the temple in Jerusalem.

    Some of those sacrifices were offered to appease a judging God

    in order to receive forgiveness for sins committed.

But eventually God sent his Son to die on the cross as the perfect sacrifice,

    the sacrifice which is the perfect substitute for animal sacrifice,

    and the perfect substitute for the sacrifice of sinful people.

Seeing this, God would be satisfied and offer forgiveness

    for those who "believe in Jesus."


Although these concepts are still prevalent in the church today,

    it's time to rethink the meaning of the "sacrifice of the cross."

How is it possible to think that the God whose name is Love

    needed his "Son" to be killed as a sacrifice to himself

    in order to overcome his anger

    and be able to forgive the sins of humanity?

This needs to be exposed as a corruption

    of the belief in a God of changeless love.

# A SECOND LOOK AT SACRIFICE (2)

So if we are dissatisfied with the substitutionary atonement approach
> to the bitter suffering and death of Jesus,
> let us see how his contemporaries interpreted
> this seeming defeat on the cross.
> Finally, let me share some alternate thoughts.

First, remember that Jesus and his followers were Jews,
> to the end imbued with the faith of Judaism,
> in which the sacrifice of animals
> was part of their temple worship.
Thus it was not strange that the Jewish people
> who were devoted to Jesus
> should see the death of their Master
> as a sublime culmination of and reversal of
> the whole system of ritual sacrifice.
Jesus the Messiah was killed. His followers saw that
> in this act he was finishing the "old covenant"
> between God and humanity
> and starting a "new covenant" based on his life and death.

Secondly, this death was indeed a sacrifice,
> but it was not offered to God but to humanity.
> Jesus was crucified because
> he had given his whole life to show people
> a better way than legalistic nit-picking,
> which Judaism had come to be.
This determination to reform Judaism
> brought him into conflict with the authorities,

beginning early in his ministry,

with escalating conflict until he was finally killed.

The sacrifice involved is clear:

Jesus sacrificed everything, even his life,

to demonstrate humanity a better way of life,

a way that was truly honest to God through total dedication,

even if it meant his eventual death.

He gave up everything, and in so doing expressed

the profound, sacrificial love of God for humanity.

# IS CHRISTIANITY EXCLUSIVE?

Jesus once said, "I am the way, the Truth and the Life;

    no one comes to the Father but by me."[xxvii]

Throughout history these words have thrown the cloak of

    exclusivism over Christianity,

        implying that all religions besides Christianity

        lead only to destruction.


Let's take another look at that.

Remember first of all that these words are not lifted from a lecture

    on comparative religion or theology;

        they were words spoken in the context of a conversation.

So what was the context?

    They were spoken to ordinary fisherman and village folk,

        who were being led astray by many "false prophets" of the day.

And they were also spoken to priests and teachers of the Law,

    many of whom were ritualistically pious but inwardly corrupt.

When Jesus said, "No one comes to the Father but by me,"

    he was drawing a contrast between his humble walk with God

    and courage to follow the spirit of the Mosaic Law,

and to follow the way of justice taught by the Hebrew prophets,

    even in the face of fierce opposition.

Jesus' words drew a contrast between the corrupt stance

    of religious leaders around him,

    who were disparaging the true spirit of Judaism

    through their self-serving, deceitful ways.


In contrast to those hypocritical teachers of the Law

    and the false prophets who were actually leading the masses astray,

Jesus proclaims "I am the Way....Don't follow those corrupt teachers;
none of them will lead you to God.
Just follow *my* way of integrity, humility, and love."

# PENTECOST

Although this Section is focusing on trinitarian ideas of Father, Son and Holy Spirit
  constituting the nature of God, we are deliberately omitting
  a lengthy discussion of the "Holy Spirit."
Church folks conveniently place the Holy Spirit as coming in flames upon
  the apostles of Jesus on the Jewish feast day called "Pentecost,"
  about a month after the Easter event.[xxviii]
Jesus had promised to send his spirit after he departed.
  Here it was! It marked the "birthday"
  of what came to be known as the Christian Church.
Simple and clear as that: God sent the Holy Spirit on Pentecost
  and it has remained as the life of the church ever since then.
  But wait a minute!
  Let's follow up in the next pages with a few questions.

# AMBIGUITIES IN THE SPIRIT (1)

We have to admit that ambiguities surround the concept of
    this "third person of the Trinity."
Much of what we have said about the Father and the Son
    is in fact describing the function of what traditional theology
    labels the "Holy Spirit."
Consider this: the creation story found in the very first verses of the Bible[xxix]
    says that the Spirit moved upon the face of the formless and desolate waters
    and the creation process began.
The Bible presents the Spirit as being present and active from the beginning,
    long before Jesus appeared on the scene.

Or consider this: Jesus had long conversations with his friends
    before his crucifixion, promising he would give them his Spirit.
After the resurrection, Jesus appeared to his followers, breathed on them,
    and said, "Receive the Holy Spirit."[xxx]
It becomes clear that what was termed the "Holy Spirit"
    was that of himself which Jesus imparted to his followers at his departure.

Or consider this: we interchangeably use
    the word "God" and "Spirit of God,"
    and we also use the word "Christ"
    and "Spirit of Christ" interchangeably.
So even in the Bible it is impossible to find a specific definition
    of a particular Being called the Holy Spirit.

# AMBIGUITIES IN THE SPIRIT (2)

I hear you saying, "This Trinity business is getting awfully complicated!"
    To which I must respond, "Yes,
        God, as Christians understand God, can be very complicated."
        So just a few more lines before we move on to more "practical" matters.

One way to answer this profound question of the function of the Holy Spirit
        is to see the Holy Spirit as the mediator
        between the Father and the Son.
And if we think of God as the ultimate transcendent One,
        and if we think of the human Jesus Christ representing
        the ultimately immanent one in human history,
then we might say that the Holy Spirit
        stands between the transcendence and immanence of God.
As such, the Spirit brings both the glory of the Creator and the teaching of Jesus
        into the everyday life of all who are open to it.

A contemporary alternative way of expressing this meaning
        of the Holy Spirit is to use the term "Cosmic Christ"—
the Spirit of Christ/the Spirit of God at work in both the
        beginning and the ending of the human story.

# THE BREATH OF GOD

There is one more aspect of the Spirit

    that is especially understandable and beautiful.

    That is the Hebrew word for spirit, *ruach,*

    a word packed with significant and down-to-earth meaning.

*Ruach* actually has three meanings: spirit, breath, and wind.

    If "spirit" is too abstract and vague in talking about God,

    we can try "breath" or "wind."


Thus it is legitimate to think of the Holy Spirit as

    the life-giving Breath of God.

Or, saying it differently, the Holy Spirit is

    the powerful Wind of God blowing through the universe.

Whenever I feel the sacred Mystery impinging on my life

    like a breeze blowing through my hair

    there is the Holy Spirit at work.

# V.

# A BIBLICAL PERSPECTIVE, WITH
# A MYSTIC'S RESPONSE<sup>xxxi</sup>

*This final section is fully open to a biblical perspective on God. Depending on your religious orientation, you might find this section offensive, too conservative and "churchy." Others will find it the most relevant and helpful section, because it contains familiar Christian, biblical views, embedded here in some new perspectives.*

*What follows are further facets of what I wish to share about my understanding of the Sacred Mystery and how I am responding to it at this point in my life. The perplexing questions are still there, but, to use a phrase, there is light at the end of the tunnel. Using the resources of sacred scriptures, my final search is to find an appropriate response to the God of grace. Yes, I believe this exploration into the nature of God would be useless were it not connected with our responses, i.e., what difference does the presence of God make in everyday life?*

*This inevitably brings us into the realm of mystical experience. The Christian "believer" has to be a person with a degree of openness to mysticism. How else can one believe Something/Someone whom no human being has ever seen? I have had a certain affinity with mysticism all my life, and have recently affirmed the mystical approach in my own religious journey, to the point where I include in the title of this section "A Mystic's Response." At the same time I acknowledge that people who have lived their life in a different context, or who have a contrasting personality type may be on a different but parallel track of faith.*

# A SONG FROM THE BIBLE [xxxii]

"Where could I go to escape from you?

    Where could I get away from your presence?

If I went up to heaven, you would be there;

    if I lay down in the world of the dead, you would be there.

If I flew away beyond the east

    or lived in the farthest place in the west,

You would be there to lead me,

    you would be there to help me.

I could ask the darkness to hide me

    or the light round me to turn into night,

but even darkness is not dark for you,

    and the night is as bright as the day.

    Darkness and light are the same to you."

This beautiful Psalm speaks for itself

    about the universal presence of God in the world.

# THE INVISIBLE GOD

From the first page to the last,

    the Jewish and Christian Scriptures proclaim

    one, invisible, holy God who alone is to be worshiped.

    It sees God as that invisible, intangible Force

    at the heart of all creation.

Many people and cultures worship

    some visible part of the universe.

It is easier to worship something tangible—

    an object, a person, a nation.

But from the earliest Hebrew history this unseen Voice

    called our forefathers in the faith

    to go deeper to connect with the hidden Mystery.

The primary essence of the Judeo-Christian God is

    that the object of worship is the *invisible* God,

    a *spiritual* God by which the whole universe exists.

Absolutely no visible thing can be regarded as the Ultimate.

    This truth troubles the rational mind,

    but also is the source of awe for the seeking soul.

# GOD—OUT-POURING LOVE<sup>xxxiii</sup>

If you were asked, What is the single most important thing in Christian faith,
   what would your answer be?
I believe the essence of Christian faith is recognizing
   the Sacred Mystery to be a *loving* God,
   or to use another word from the biblical tradition, a God of *grace.*
This out-pouring love finds its focus in belief
   in the *kenosis* (Greek for "emptying") of God,
   which refers especially to the love of the Christ for the world shown
   in his final act of "emptying" his life for others on the cross of his death.
Whatever philosophical concepts we may use to define the sacred Mystery—
   all this is secondary to the recognition that the divine entity
   is characterized by an oceanic outpouring we experience as love.

This is a love that makes the world we know
   to be a benevolent place if we but have eyes to see it.
This benevolence provides the impulse
   for all living things to grow and develop,
It is a benevolence that accepts human beings as we are,
   and challenges us into a better tomorrow.
This is the "amazing grace" about which we love to sing.

# THE ETERNAL PARADOX:
## TRANSCENDENCE vs. IMMANENCE[xxxiv]

When we contemplate the vastness of the universe and the sacred Mystery,

    it seems preposterous to believe that this God

    is the very object of my everyday faith.

The fundamental paradox, which we have already encountered many times, is:

    *How can God be both transcendent and immanent at once?*

    Transcendent—being exalted far above and beyond us;

    immanent—being present within us.

Can I myself actually be in touch with the Holy Mystery,

    who existed "before the foundations of the world were laid"? Impossible!

But no, this One is the very intimate "Abba" (Father, "Papa") of Jesus.


Does the concept of "Trinity" add light to this point?

    The Holy Spirit is called the "Comforter" and the "Counselor,"

    words that describe intimate relationship and help.

The Gospel of John often speaks of this mystery,

    as when Jesus prays to God for his followers thus:

"I in them and you in me, so that they may be completely one . . .

    so the world may know...that you love them as you love me."[xxxv]

# IS GOD OMNIPOTENT?<sup>xxxvi</sup>

Christian creeds speak of God as being almighty, all powerful, omnipotent.

> But there is a problem inherent in this statement:
>
> If God is all powerful, why does God allow
>
> natural catastrophes and fatal diseases?

If God is omnipotent, this is a question that begs an answer.

> This concept of God drives many away from Christianity.

But remember the overwhelming story of God's *kenosis,*

> which is at the heart of the whole New Testament:

That is, God gave up the divine glory to reveal the divine self

> in becoming a vulnerable man.

Theologian Thomas Oord entitles his recent book, *God Can't.*

> John Cobb's view is that God is neither omnipotent,
>
> nor in control of human behavior.

To think that God controls the stars and planets and you and me

> is an absurd notion, and quite unnecessary
>
> to accompany the belief in a God of creative love.

The magnificent creation is a vulnerable creation,

> open to possible disease, disaster, or destruction at any time.
>
> God does not, cannot keep it in "perfect condition" all the time.

And Christians believe that God created mankind with freedom.

> When that element is "added to the mix," endless complexities arise.

# WHAT IS THE "IMAGE OF GOD"

We can swim with abandon in safe waters

    when we believe that God is not a *Being* among other beings,

    but truly the fullness of Reality, the water in which we by nature swim.


God is the dynamic process of development of this evolving universe,

    in which we share responsibility with God for continued growth.

The Bible says that we are created in the "image of God."

    This is indeed a pregnant phrase.

    How are we like God? How is God like us? A huge subject!

    I believe we are continuing *co-creators* with God

    striving to continue to develop our own potential as a human being,

    also striving continuously to create wonderful things

    out of the materials of the world given us to use.


"Image of God" is also a phrase with universal application.

    It is a basis for mutual human respect and cooperation.

For instance, it is sheer ugly pride to think that

    any one race or clan has a larger claim than another to that image.

    The divine image applies to the whole human race or to no one.

# THE LURE OF GOD

I have stumbled at the concept of God being a God

    who proactively reveals God's self,

    who communicates with human beings.

We have tried to see God as the Sacred Mystery of love and creativity.

We can communicate ourselves to others, as we constantly do,

    in various ways and with greater or lesser effectiveness.

    So why is it a surprise that the Creator does as much as the creatures do?

The divine word becomes a call to those who have ears to hear.

In my experience, that word lures us forward, calling us

    to enjoy the experience of intimacy with the divine Self.

It calls us to be ourselves, the self we were from birth created to be.

    It challenges us to be creators, using the materials around us.

    It invites us to a life of receiving and giving love.

# THE SPEAKING GOD

Consider how the God worshiped in all the Abrahamic faiths
    is seen as a God who *speaks*.
The Bible from beginning to end is about a speaking God,
    communicating through "prophets," through Jesus, the Messiah,
    and through those who listen for "the Voice" throughout the ages.
    "God is still speaking" is the meaningful logo of the United Church of Christ.

However, this is not to say that God is like a human person
    speaking from some invisible corner of the heavens.
I am attracted to the title of Chet Raymo's book,
    *When God is Gone, Everything is Holy.* [xxxvii]
    That person sitting somewhere in the heavens is gone.
Rather, as the book title suggests,
    God is the sacred which exists in all creation,
And through awakened consciousness and conscience
    we hear this God speaking through the world around us
    as well as in the recesses of our heart.

A psalm attributed to King David says it beautifully:
    "The heavens declare the glory of God
    and the firmament shows His handiwork;
    Day unto day utters speech
    and night unto night reveals knowledge." [xxxviii]

# A FORGIVING GOD

Why is it important to see God as forgiving?

Look at it this way: Human beings were created with a self-preservation instinct.

> We feel we must ward off attack—physical or verbal—by others.

> If we didn't have that instinct we would soon cease to exist.

However, the design of creation is for us to live

> in peaceful harmony with all,

> to love the neighbor as oneself,

> even to relinquish ones own benefit for the sake of others.

But our primal instinct for preservation of self collides

> in absolute conflict with giving up ones self for others.

> This conflict is the root of wrong-doing we call sin.

"Forgiveness of sin" is the divine Voice saying, "I understand.

> You need to preserve yourself, but it's not OK to be primarily self-centered,

> because that's the root of evil in human society

> which throws both individuals and nations into conflict and chaos.

But if you regretfully recognize this, you are accepted anyway.

> So turn your face toward me and I will show you a better way,

> the way of forgiving love among yourselves."

That is the beautiful process of forgiveness of sin and transformation.

# THE IMMANENT GOD—"WITH US"[xxxix]

We claim that God is always with us, and yet life goes on,
    usually in a ho-hum, hum-drum, "business as usual" manner.
    Bad things continually happen to good people.
    Needy people pray for blessing, but they remain poor.
How do we make sense of this, in a way that shows our faith in God
    is not just naiveté and in the end only an illusion?

We are forced to rethink the nature of divine activity,
    the nature of the God who is always "with us."
If life is 98% hum-drum while at the same time
    we believe God is with us always,
    then God must be part of the hum-drum itself.

But normal people can handle the hum-drum aspects of life themselves.
    We don't need a revelation of special divine power
    to help us brush our teeth, or to eat dinner.
Yet we do believe that God is always there
    in the dynamic process of the hum-drum itself.
If we live in that awareness, when shock or tragedy strike, we have a buffer.
    We recognize that the God who is always with us
    is our faithful source of hope and encouragement.

The crux is, am I open to the presence of God
    being always with me?
When I am, there is transformation
    of hum-drum into creativity and joy,
    and spiritual strength in times of distress.

# THE CREATING GOD

By this time you may be wondering why
    God as creator has not been in front center stage.
The common notion of God and God's function in the large picture
    is that God is the creator of the universe.
Whether God is anything else or not, at least this is the One
    who created this marvelous world and human life.
However, is not this the very point where two worlds
    have been in conflict for more than a century?

Ever since the publication of Charles Darwin's
    *On the Origin of the Species* in 1859,
    modern scientific culture has been captivated by the idea that everything—
    plants, animals, human beings—developed over billions of years
    by the process of natural selection.
There was no God who created by a divine word.
    Therefore the old concept of God as creator is outmoded.
This kind of scientific approach to the natural and social world
    is the general assumption on which our present-day culture is built.

How do Christians deal with this view which is in stark contrast
    to the biblical acknowledgement of creation by God?
We will make no attempt to argue creationism vs. evolution,
    but recently more people, myself included, are asking prior questions:
If our universe came into being in one "Big Bang,"
    from where did the energy of the Big Bang come?
What is the source of gravity
    that holds the stars and planets in place?
    What is the origin of light? Of electricity? Of life?

The evolutionary process can no longer be denied.

But I believe there is a sacred Presence

    beyond the evolution described by science.

Even after Darwin, God is not dead!

# HIDDEN IN "LIGHT INACCESSIBLE"

Is God revealed in the Scriptures?

>  The blithe answer of most Christians is, "Of course."

>  But consider the many places in the Old Testament

>  where God's people cry out,

"How much longer will you forget me, Lord? Forever?

>  How much longer will you hide yourself from me?"[xl]

And in the New Testament there are

>  those heart-rending words of Jesus on the cross,

>  "My God, my God, why have you forsaken me!"

Theologians through the centuries have spoken of God

>  as *Deus absconditus* (hidden God)

>  along with *Deus revelatus* (revealed God).

A frequently used hymn to sing at the opening of a worship service is

>  "Immortal, invisible, God only wise,

>  in light inaccessible hid from our eyes . . ."

In my experience God is more often hidden and inaccessible

>  than revealed and "available."

>  So we must continue the painful journey with *Deus absconditus.*

Blaise Pascal once said that

>  a religion which does not see God as a hidden God is not a true religion.

# "I DON'T KNOW"

When the Spirit seems close, the heart melts with fervent longing, God is near—

   What happy times these are!

But when the spiritual awareness wanes, the heart grows cold, and God seems absent.

   We feel, "I can't believe in God; maybe there is a God, maybe not."

That is the time to let the apostle Thomas empathize with us. He dared to say:

   "Unless I see the scars of the nails in his hands

   and put my finger on those scars

   and my hand in his side, I will not believe."[xli]


Good science and good religion both start with "I don't know."

As a youth, I read a devotional book by the great preacher, E. Stanley Jones.

   The first prayer in his book startled me,

   but has often been in my prayers through the years:

   "O God, if there be a God . . ."


It's all right to question and doubt—doubt is the back side of faith.

   Doubt digs deeper into the dark unknown, seeking the light.

   Doubt does not mean closing the door of mind and heart;

   It is searching for the possibility

   of a new understanding of the Sacred Mystery.

# THE EMBODIED GOD

I'm coming to see the Sacred Mystery

    not as the king of the universe, but as the breath of life,

    as the energy in all things,

    as the fountain of meaning.

I seek eagerly for the gut-level experience,

    the experience of holding a joyful faith in a loving God.


But where can I meet this God?

    If God exists in all the stuff of the universe,

    then this God can also be found in my own mind and body.

    Yes, God's Spirit is *embodied in me.*

Perhaps the Spirit is like an alter-ego (*ego* meaning the *self),*

    a counterpart to the self I was born with,

    the conscience with which I dialogue all day long.


The Spirit needs a form for the formless, it needs my human body,

    and it needs a billion bodies to dance through history!

Significantly, St. Paul called our body

    "the temple of the living God."[xlii]

# DIVE IN!

Through the many pages of this book we have sought to
     discover the meaning of God as the Sacred Mystery
     throughout the universe, throughout human life.
We have even found God communicating with us,
     luring us upward, calling us forward.
But this story would be incomplete without a last step.

The call of the mysterious Presence awaits a response.
     I believe I speak for myself and many others
     who know this talk about God already,
     who perhaps sit in the same pew every Sunday morning.
Many of us walk around the mystic pool of grace,
     seeing it as a beautiful body of water,
     ruminating about the great feel of being in the water,
     but hesitating to dive in.
Why do we fear to take the dive into the depths of spirituality
     to feel the joy of total immersion,
     to allow the water of the Spirit to buoy us up?

Cogitation and rationality, abundant in this book,
     are poor substitutes for the real thing.
Thinking about the pool is theology; diving into the pool is faith—
     the difference between talking *about* God and talking *to* God.
The first is an academic exercise;
     the latter is a mystical experience.
Theologizing demands intellect;
     diving in demands courage.

# THE "EARTHY" WILL OF GOD

We pray, "Thy will be done on earth." Yes, on earth.

    That will—the way of God—is not something heavenly—it's "earthy"!

When we pray "Thy will be done" we are prone to turn our minds

    toward abstract "spirituality."

    But the phrase "on earth" points not toward spiritual abstractions

    but to my everyday earthly and earthy activities.

The "will of God"—What is it? Who can know it?

    This is a "trick question" which cannot be answered glibly.

    When friends talk as though they exactly know the will of God

    I feel an air of arrogance.

The only way I can know the will of God is when

    I seek to follow the way of living exemplified by Jesus,

    walking in love and justice,

    and using my capacity for creative work.

Is it not simply living mindfully in the "now,"

    being open to the still, small voice of the Spirit,

    and doing what needs to be done now?

# JESUS, TEMPLATE OF THE KINGDOM OF GOD

The New Testament frequently uses the phrase, "Kingdom of God"

    to describe the way God works in the world,

        especially through the divinely appointed One, Jesus, the "Messiah."

    It describes the kind of life God desires for all people.

The Kingdom of God is not a political entity, but a way of life.

    The early designation of Christians was "people of the Way."

What is that essence? It is the way of life

    taught by and lived out by Jesus of Nazareth—

    the way of sacrificial love, the way of healing,

    the way of justice but also forgiveness,

    the way of constant openness to the Father's voice—

    this is the Kingdom of God.

This Kingdom of God is present today wherever there is

    inclusive insistence on justice for all.

It is the way of mutually compassionate forgiveness.

    It is the life that emulates the template of Jesus.

# HOW CAN WE RELATE TO THE MYSTERY?

All this talk about God and Jesus might well be in vain,

    merely an intellectual exercise,

    unless there is some human response to this God.

The study of theology can be nothing more than academic verbiage

    unless the relevance of God-talk to human experience is acknowledged.

Is it possible for us to maintain a conscious relationship

    with the Transcendent One?

Let's look at this question from the negative side:

What really separates us from God is that

    in spite of knowing that this One

    cares for the whole creation, including myself,

    we doubt this; we despair.

We get depressed and say, "I have no place to turn for help;

    there is no love in the universe; life is meaningless."

    This rejects the unconditional grace offered by the Sacred Mystery.

The spirit of expectancy, trust, openness and gratitude

    creates a divine-human relationship and keeps it alive.

# TRANSFORMATION

St. Paul once wrote of his behavior in paradoxical terms, saying:

    "It is no longer I who live, but it is Christ who lives in me."[xliii]

This is the kind of paradox that arises out of the mystical experience

    of the *ruach,* (Hebrew language for the divine "breath" within us.)


It is experiencing everyday activities to be like a machine

    all wired up for action,

    but without any electric current in the wires.

Then the current, the Mystery, begins to flow,

    and creative work can be done.

Or it is like a valuable piece of art we came to see,

    but we find it hanging in a darkened room, unseen.

    Then the light is turned on and

    all is transformed; the beauty of the art inspires us.


The divine Spirit is utterly non-material and hidden,

    yet it mysteriously changes everything—like electricity, like light.

My prayer is that I may be open to the flow of this life energy

    into myself and through me to others.

# A PRAYER: TOUCH ME!

God, I sense you are the Sacred Mystery

in the grandeur of creation embracing me.

But I long for a deeper encounter with the living "Thou."

You who dwell in the heights of heaven

and in the depths of the human soul,

You who are known most clearly in the cosmic Spirit of Christ,

who brought healing to the infirm and life to the dead,

who brings wholeness to the humble heart—

I believe You are here.

So touch me now, and

bring peace, bring joy,

bring new life to my longing spirit!

# ENDNOTES

## I. Is a New Paradigm Possible?

i.   See the scholarly work of Gordon Kaufman in *God the Problem,* chap. 1.

ii.  Psalm 13:1-2.

iii. Mayfield, Rich, in *A Case for Christian Atheism,* in *Alive and Well and Talking Jesus, Vol* 8, 82–83.

iv.  See Reginald Stackhouse, *The God Nobody Knows,* for a book that deals with the same kind of questions we do here.

v.   See Mark 2:21–22.

vi.  I Corinthians 3:16.

vii. Exodus 3:14

viii. See *Schilling, God in an Age of Atheism,* where he quotes Richard Rubenstein, a Jewish rabbi, commenting on the holocaust: "The thread uniting God and man, heaven and earth, has been broken." 123.

ix.  For a fuller treatment of God as an uncontrolling God, see Thomas Jay Oord, *God Can't.*

## II. Metaphors Pointing to God

x.   I am indebted to Prof. Thomas Moore of Pomona College for clarity on the subject of gravity.

xi.  For a full treatment of this subject see Sally McFague, *The Body of God.*

xii. Charles Bayer, "Do We Still Need Religion?" Lecture given at Pilgrim Place, May 4, 2016, 3.

xiii. Ephesians 5:31–32.

xiv. Soelle, Chap. 2, gives a critique of the concept of God as "father" from a feminist perspective.

## III. God, the Sacred Mystery

xv.  For a review of philosophical approaches to God, see R. T. Allen, *The Necessity of God.*

xvi.     For a full treatment of this subject see the writings of Paul Tillich, 20th century German theologian who had strong influence on American theology, especially during his years at Union Theological Seminary in New York.

xvii.    Panentheism is defined as "the belief that the divine pervades and interpenetrates every part of the universe and also extends beyond time and space." Wikipedia.

xviii.   Harrington, Joel, *Dangerous Mystic: Eckhart's Path to the God Within,* quoted in a book review in Christian Century, May 23, 2018.

xix.     Borg, Marcus, *Speaking Christian*, 73.

xx.      See Charles Bayer, "My Quest for a Personal God," 20–37.

xxi.     For a full discussion of God as "Abba" see John Cobb's *Jesus' Abba.*

## IV. A Three-faced God?

xxii.    For fuller discussion and a modern interpretation of the Trinity see Richard Rohr's columns of daily readings/probing on the internet at Rohr's Center for Contemplation and Action, April-May, 2019.

xxiii.   See Richard Dawkins, *The God Delusion,* quoted by Hitchens, 287.

xxiv.    Excerpts from the extremely long "Athanasian Creed" (fifth century, but still used infrequently today) which attempted to analyze definitively exactly how Jesus and God are related.

xxv.     See John 14:8-14 for a conversation between Jesus and his disciple Philip on the unity that exists between the two.

xxvi.    Anselm, Archbishop of Canterbury in early 12 century.

xxvii.   John 14:6.

xxviii.  Acts 2:1–4.

xxix.    Genesis 1:2.

xxx.     John 20:22.

## V. A Biblical Perspective, with a mystic's response

xxxi.    For a concise overview of the traditional understanding of God in mainline Protestantism in mid-20th century U. S. A., see Stephen Neill, *The Christians' God.*

xxxii.   Psalm 139.

xxxiii.  *Kenosis* is a Greek word meaning "emptying." The classic passage in the New Testament portraying the divine *kenosis* is Philippians 2:5–10

xxxiv.   For an in-depth exploration of the mystery of God from the perspective of a Christian theologian, see Chaps. 1 and 2 of Bob Hurd, *Compassionate Christ, Compassionate People.* Hurd says that simultaneous immanence and transcendence is the classical view of the nature of God, and it is modern theism that thinks of God's transcendence as separation from creation—God "out there" somewhere, and we and our world here, with a great gulf between the two.

xxxv.    See the intimacy of this relationship spelled out in John 17.

xxxvi.   "Is God Omnipotent?" was the theme of a public debate between Stephen Davis and John Cobb at Pilgrim Place in Claremont, CA, March 18, 2019

xxxvii.  See Chet Raymo, *When God is Gone, Everything is Holy.*

xxxviii. Psalm 19:1–2.

xxxix.   One of the names ascribed to Jesus at birth was "Immanuel," which means "God with us."

xl.      Psalm 13:1.

xli.     John 20:24-29.

xlii.    I Corinthians 6:19.

xliii.   See Paul's bold words in Galatians 2:19-21.

# BIBLIOGRAPHY

Allen, R. T. *The Necessity of God*. Piscataway, NJ: Transaction Publishers, 2008.

Bayer, Charles. "Do We Still Need Religion?" Lecture at Pilgrim Place, May 4, 2016.

————. *Reclaiming the Christian Faith*. St Louis, MO: Lucas Parks, 2008.

————. "My Quest for a Personal God." In *Road Rage and Resurrection: Doing Theology at Pilgrim Place*, edited by Paul Kittlaus and Pat Patterson, Vol 5. Shelbyville, KY: Wasteland, 2010.

Borg, Marcus. *Speaking Christian: Why Christian Words Have Lost Their Meaning and Power—and How They Can be Restored*. New York: Harper One/Harper Collins, 1989.

————. *The Heart of Christianity: Rediscovering a Life of Faith*. New York: Harper SanFrancisco/Harper, 2003.

————. *Speaking Christian*. New York: Harper One, 1989.

Clayton, Philip. *Transforming Christian Theology for Church and Society*. Minneapolis: Fortress, 2010.

Cobb, John. *Jesus' Abba: The God who Has Not Failed*. Minneapolis: Fortress, 2015.

Davis, Andrew and Philip Clayton, eds. *How I Found God in Everyone and Everywhere: An Anthology of Spiritual Memoirs*. Rhinebeck, NY: Monkfish, 2018.

Dowd, Michael. *Thank God for Evolution*. New York: Penguin Group/Plume, 2007.

Geering, Lloyd. *Reimagining God*. Salem, OR: Polebridge, 2014.

Helminiak, Daniel. *What Do You Do When You Outgrow Your Religion?* N.p.: CreateSpace, 2013.

Hitchens, Christopher. *The Portable Atheist: Essential Reading for the Nonbeliever*. Boston: Da Capo, 2007.

Hurd, Bob. *Compassionate Christ, Compassionate People*. Collegeville, MN: Liturgical Press Academic, 2019.

Isherwood, Margaret. *Searching for Meaning*. London: George Allen & Unwin Ltd, 1970,

Kaufman, Gordon. *God the Problem*. Harvard University Press, 1972.

Mayfield, Rich. "A Case for Christian Atheism." In *Alive and Well and Talking Jesus, Doing Theology at Pilgrim Place*, edited by Paul Kittlaus et al., Vol. 8. Shelbyville, KY: Wasteland, 2013.

————. *Reconstructing Christianity*. Lincoln: iUniverse, 2005.

McFague, Sally. *The Body of God: an Ecological Theology*. Minneapolis: Fortress, 1993.

McLaren, Brian. *Everything Must Change: Jesus, Global Crisis and a Revolution of Hope*. Nelson: 2007.

————. *The Great Spiritual Migration: How the World's Largest Religion is Seeking a Better Way to be Christian*. New York: Convergent, 2016.

Miles, Jack. *God: A Biography*. Knopf, 1995.

Neill, Stephen. *The Christians' God*. New York: Association, 1954.

Oord, Thomas Jay. *God Can't*. Grasmere, ID: SacraSage, 2019.

————. *The Uncontrolling Love of God*. Downers Grove: IVP Academic, 2015.

Raymo, Chet. *When God is Gone Everything is Holy*. Notre Dame: Sorin, 2008.

Robinson, John. *Honest To God*. London: SCM, 1963.

Rollins, Peter. *How (Not) to Speak of God*. Brewster, MA: Paraclete, 2006.

Schilling, S. Paul. *God in an Age of Atheism*. Abingdon, 1969.

Soelle, Dorothee, *Theology for Skeptics: Reflections on God*. Minneapolis: Fortress, 1995.

Stackhouse, Reginald. *The God Nobody Knows: Unexplored Dimensions of Belief*. Toronto, Canada: Anglican Book Centre, 1986.

Stark, Rodney. *One True God: Historical Consequences of Monotheism*. Princeton University Press, 2001.